Saints
ON CALL

Everyday Devotions
For Moms

Christine

Liguori
ONE LIGUORI DRIVE
LIGUORI MO 63057-9999

Imprimi Potest: Harry Grile, CSsR, Provincial
Denver Province, The Redemptorists

Published by Liguori Publications
Liguori, Missouri 63057

To order, call 800-325-9521, or visit liguori.org

Library of Congress Cataloging-in-Publication Data

Gibson, Christine.
 Saints on call : everyday devotions for moms / Christine Gibson.—1st ed.
   p. cm.
 ISBN 978-0-7648-2034-2
 1. Mothers—Prayers and devotions. 2. Christian saints—Prayers and devotions.
 3. Catholic Church—Prayers and devotions. I. Title.
 BX2353.G53 2011
 242'.6431—dc22
                                      2011010554

Liguori Publications, a nonprofit corporation, is an apostolate of the Redemptorists. To learn more about the Redemptorists, visit Redemptorists.com.

Printed in the United States of America
15 14 13 12 11 / 5 4 3 2 1

First Edition

For my own saintly mother,
who is always on call

ACKNOWLEDGMENT

*With gratitude to my husband for his patient help
in bringing this project to fruition*

Contents

Introduction

For many years I lacked an understanding of the role of the saints in our Catholic faith tradition. Why should one pray to saints when one can pray to Jesus? I wondered. It seemed the implication was that we were too far away from Jesus for him to hear our prayers, and we would have better luck with someone "higher up" praying for us.

But some time ago, I encountered a very simple yet thought-provoking question: If we can ask our friends here on earth to pray for us, why would we hesitate to ask those who have gone before us? This gave me pause. I often asked friends to pray for me. In doing so, I never felt that I was saying that I couldn't pray to Jesus or that my friends were "higher up" than I. Would asking for the saints' prayers be any different? Could I expand my circle of friends to include the saints?

I considered that perhaps Scripture and our tradition had something to say in answer to my questions. There is some biblical basis for the idea of the angels and saints praying for us here on earth. The Book of Revelation not only mentions the "prayers of the holy ones," but through the use of imagery describes the saints in heaven offering to God the prayers of the saints on earth (Revelation 5:8). We also read a little later, in 8:4, of an angel in heaven offering the prayers of the earthly saints: "The smoke of the incense along with the prayers of the holy ones went up before God from the hand of the angel."

While Scripture doesn't exactly speak of keeping the saints "on call," interceding for our daily needs, this idea comes through in the tradition of our faith, particularly through the teachings of some of the early Church Fathers. They were clear that those who go to heaven continue to pray for their fellow Christians on earth. Saint Cyprian of Carthage (bishop and martyr) preached in the third century: "Let us on both sides [of death] always pray for one another." Encouraging Christians to pray for one another even after death, he said, "if one of us…shall go hence first, our love may continue in the presence of the Lord, and our prayers for our brethren and sisters not cease in the presence of the Father's mercy." We can rest assured that it is out of Christian love that the saints in heaven pray for us today.

If we accept that the saints in heaven can pray for us, we might next ask which saints we should call on. I never learned about the lives of many saints, so they never seemed like real people; they seemed like figures who were born as stained-glass beings. The stories of the saints are fascinating, and we can find that many faced situations, trials, and burdens very similar to those we encounter today. Others led lives entirely different from ours, but we can often find some aspect of their spirituality or their story that resonates with us. My chief desire in writing this book is to help readers discover that although they may have always had a special devotion to a particular saint, they can relate to many more saints than they may have imagined, in many more situations of daily life than they thought possible.

For moms, each day brings new needs, new concerns, and new prayer requests. I know this from experience, so I've designed this book with these things in mind. The table of contents is organized to help you quickly find the saint whose prayers you may need at any particular time. Once you find your saint to call, you can turn to her entry to learn more about this woman of faith, and learn from her life through a short reflection. Each reflection takes but a few minutes to read and is followed by a Scripture verse and prayer.

I hope this book provides you with the encouragement and comfort you are seeking.

CHAPTER 1

Everyday Challenges

When you suffer in any way...

Saint Mary, sister of Lazarus

Saint Mary, sister of Lazarus and Martha, was a good friend of Jesus. She is known to us as the one who sat at the feet of Jesus while her sister, Martha, busied herself with hostess duties and as the one who was upset that Jesus did not come to save Lazarus from death.

I yearned for a baby for years. All of our best efforts at conceiving failed. Month after month, we faced the same disappointment. Our adoption process proved difficult as well, as months of waiting turned into years.

What do we do, what do we think, when, contrary to Scripture, we ask and we do not receive, we knock and the door remains firmly closed?

Mourning the death of her brother, Lazarus, Mary says to Jesus, "If you had been here, my brother would not have died." Isn't that what we want to say when that door refuses to budge? "Jesus, if you were here, if you cared, I would have a child/I would find a job/this depression would lift/my child would be cured."

Maybe Mary is showing us that it's OK to share with Jesus our hurt, our disappointment, and our frustration. Although we would like to be able to calmly say, "Thy will be done," in the face of sorrow, Jesus is there when we can't. In fact, the Bible tells us that when Jesus saw Lazarus in the tomb, he wept. He shared in Mary's sorrow, just as he can share in ours.

Come to me, all you who labor and are burdened, and I will give you rest.
MATTHEW 11:28

Saint Mary, please pray that I may find comfort in knowing that Jesus shares in my sorrow, and may I ever have hope that a miracle awaits me as it did you.

When you feel "sacrificed out" for your family…

Saint Gianna Molla

Saint Gianna lived in Italy from 1922–1962. She was a devout Catholic, a wife, mother, and physician. Gianna died after delivering her third child, whom her doctor recommended she abort in order to save her own life. She is the patron of mothers and physicians, and her feast day is April 28.

Every mother sacrifices for her children. One sacrifice that many of us struggle with is lost sleep. Perhaps we used to be eight-hour-a-night beauty-sleep believers, but motherhood makes us yearn for a good six-hour stretch. There are other sacrifices as well—extra cash, date nights with our husbands, lunches with girlfriends, tidy, quiet homes, leisurely mornings.…

Once in a while (particularly after some serious sleep deprivation), we may feel a little "sacrificed out." "What about my needs?" we want to ask as we tend to everyone else's.

Saint Gianna Molla is someone to turn to when that "sacrificed out" feeling emerges. Gianna was two months pregnant with her third child when she was diagnosed with a uterine tumor. She was given three options for treatment, but only one would allow her to continue to carry her unborn baby. A physician herself, Gianna chose this option knowing that it was the most dangerous for her own health, as difficulties could arise at delivery. As her pregnancy continued, Gianna informed physicians and family that if a choice had to be made to save her or the baby, they must save the baby.

Unfortunately, such a decision had to be made. Gianna gave birth to a healthy baby girl, Gianna Emmanuella, but she herself died eight days later.

Gianna's example of the ultimate sacrifice for her children can help us see the big and small sacrifices we make each day in a new light.

Each must do as already determined, without sadness or compulsion, for God loves a cheerful giver.
2 CORINTHIANS 9:7

Saint Gianna, you made the ultimate sacrifice for your little one. I ask you to please pray for me that I may rejoice in the sacrifices that I can make for my dear children.

When you are exhausted by mundane tasks…

Saint Veronica

Saint Veronica is known as the woman from Jerusalem who wiped Jesus' face as he struggled toward Calvary. This act is depicted in the Sixth Station of the Cross. Tradition says that Christ's face was imprinted on her cloth. She is the patron saint of photographers and laundry workers. Her feast day is July 12.

It has been said that you can sum up a mother's job with two words: She wipes. Whether it be countertops, baby bottoms, noses, faces, tables, or toys, mothers are constant wipers. This can feel so monotonous, insignificant, and tedious! And many of us wipers are women who were accustomed to (in a former life) or are accustomed to (during the 9-to-5 time frame) making important corporate decisions, managing major meetings of the minds, and other activities that may seem to matter more. How could God want us to spend our time wiping?

When you're weary after wiping that same sticky little toddler face for the tenth time, or at your wit's end from comforting a fussy baby all day, consider Saint Veronica.

In the midst of the passion, Saint Veronica stepped into the crowd to offer the only comfort she could: She wiped the face of the suffering Christ. This small, seemingly insignificant act is represented in the Sixth Station of the Cross, allowing the faithful throughout the ages to contemplate the compassion and tenderness that Veronica brought to the heart-wrenching scene.

Recall Jesus' words recorded in Matthew 25:40. "Whatever you did for one of these least brothers of mine, you did for me." Those monotonous, insignificant, tedious tasks that you perform for the little ones, you perform for him.

For I was hungry and you gave me food, I was thirsty and you gave me drink, a stranger and you welcomed me, naked and you clothed me, ill and you cared for me, in prison and you visited me.
MATTHEW 25:35–36

Saint Veronica, please pray for me as I perform a million seemingly inconsequential tasks today. Please pray that I, like you, will provide comfort when I am needed and that I may catch a glimpse of the sacred in the mundane.

When you are shy about expressing your faith…

The "Sinful Woman"

"She…began to bathe his feet with her tears. Then she wiped them with her hair, kissed them, and anointed them with the ointment" (Luke 7:38).

Sometimes we're timid about making the sign of the cross in public, or we're hesitant to refer to or defend our Catholic faith in certain circles. We might think about this fellow sinner's response to Jesus when we feel shy or awkward expressing our own faith.

The woman in this passage is known only as a "sinful woman," though in John's Gospel she is identified as Mary Magdalene. She entered the Pharisee's house, not because she was invited, but because she was a bold follower of Christ. Then she began her extravagant, loving, and humble act of washing his feet with her tears. Again, no shame, no apology, no timidity, just love, adoration, and the desire to be forgiven.

We don't know what her sin was, nor do we care. As sinners just like her, we're interested in her emotional, loving, public adoration of the one who will forgive her. And we long for the courage to follow her example.

He said to him, "You shall love the Lord, your God, with all your heart, with all your soul, and with all your mind."
MATTHEW 22:37

Dear Mary Magdalene: I am inspired by your public adoration at the feet of Jesus. Please pray that I may worship my Lord with abandon.

When you feel like an outcast…

The hemorrhaging woman

In this famous Gospel episode in Luke 8, crowds are pressing in on Jesus, but he feels the "power go out" of himself when the hemorrhaging woman grabs his clothing. He recognizes her great faith and says that it is this faith that has healed her.

Cast out, isolated, lonely. At some point we may feel that these labels describe us. For whatever reason, we find ourselves on the outside hardly daring to look in.

The hemorrhaging woman was an outcast in her society. Mosaic law stated that as a result of her hemorrhage (of twelve years) she was unclean and unfit for human contact. Luke tells us that she had spent her life savings seeking a cure. So there she was, ill, outcast, and impoverished. And there he was, her only hope.

As Jesus was going through town with throngs of people surrounding him, she made her way close enough to touch his cloak. She, whom society had cast out as "untouchable," reached out and touched divinity. She hung onto him with such faith that she was cured. Jesus told her, "Daughter, your faith has saved you."

When we are at our lowest, our loneliest, our most isolated, may we, too, grab hold of him. His words tell us that if we fly to him for our cure, we will be healed.

Look upon me, have pity on me, for I am alone and afflicted.
PSALM 25:16

Nameless woman, your faith is a model to us all. Please pray that in my time of desolation, I may reach out to him who heals.

When you feel rejected...

Saint Margaret of Castello

Saint Margaret lived in Italy in the fourteenth century. Although Margaret was born with several disabilities and was abandoned by her parents, she persevered in a life of holiness and service. She is the patron of the unborn and those born with disabilities, and her feast day is April 13.

All of us know something about feeling rejected or abandoned. Perhaps our dearest friends whom we admire and love are nowhere to be found when we need them most. Maybe we've been abandoned by our husbands and left to raise children on our own. Whatever the situation, we feel alone, hurt, and unloved. We may wonder how we can be any good to anyone when we are experiencing such anguish.

Saint Margaret of Castello was born crippled and blind, a complete embarrassment to her parents, who hid her away in a cell in their castle. At one point, they heard that their daughter might be cured if they took her on a pilgrimage to a church in Castello. Finding no cure, they abandoned young Margaret right there in the church.

By God's grace, Margaret was taken in by a devout local couple who found her wandering the streets. Soon she entered religious life, eventually focusing her ministry on works of mercy for the poor and imprisoned. Perhaps we can follow Margaret's example of using our own pain and feelings of rejection as a catalyst for loving the unloved of this world.

For the Lord will not forsake his people, nor abandon his inheritance.
Psalm 94:14

Saint Margaret, please pray that I may remember my own feelings of loneliness, rejection, and hurt, only so that I may better serve those who suffer today.

When you feel inadequate…

The Poor Widow

One of the few individuals whom Jesus specifically praises, the "poor widow" described in the Gospels of Mark and Luke is honored for giving all that she had.

I can sing a little, but I'm probably not good enough for the church choir. I've taught before, but I'm probably not as good as some of the others. They could find someone better for religious education classes. I'm not really knowledgeable enough to start up a Bible study.…

Do these phrases sound familiar? Some of us are really good at minimizing our strengths until we convince ourselves that we are completely inadequate and have nothing whatsoever to offer anybody. Compared to this person or that, we aren't as good, aren't as talented, and so on.

There is a woman in the Gospels who had little to contribute as well. The poor widow of the Gospels of Mark and Luke contributes "two small coins" to the treasury, much less than what the wealthy folks around her were giving. She could have told herself, "I just don't have much to contribute. I can't be of much use." But she didn't. She said to herself, "I don't have much, but I'll give all I have." And how did Jesus respond to this gesture? He said, "…this poor widow put in more than all the rest." To him, she was the most generous, even though she had the least to give.

Maybe that is how Jesus responds when we give all that we have. Even when we're sure it isn't much. He doesn't judge us for our level of talent, wealth, or ability, but it seems he does judge us for our willingness to share what we have been given.

She, from her poverty, has offered her whole livelihood.
LUKE 21:4

When you feel overwhelmed...

Saint Elizabeth Ann Seton

Born in the United States in 1774, Saint Elizabeth Ann Seton was the first native-born American to be canonized. A mother, widow, and convert to Catholicism, Saint Elizabeth devoted herself to a life of faithful service to children, founding schools and orphanages. She is the patron of widows, against the death of children and parents, and those ridiculed for their faith. Her feast day is January 4.

The joys of motherhood are innumerable. What few people tell you is that the stressors and anxieties are as well. Illness, marital problems, financial woes, moves, and all the pressures of a regular life are intensified because of our love for the little ones.

Sometimes these and other pressures make us feel that we're too overwhelmed to accomplish anything at all. As tempting as it is, we can't give in to this feeling. Others with equally challenging situations have persevered through God's grace.

Saint Elizabeth Ann Seton, mother of five, was widowed at age twenty-eight. Her husband's business had failed, leaving the family bankrupt. On top of it all, she, an American, had moved to Italy hoping the climate would cure her ailing husband. In mourning, facing single parenthood to five children (all under the age of eight!), Elizabeth found herself with no husband and no money in a foreign country.

How did she escape feeling paralyzed and overwhelmed? How did she even manage to put one foot in front of the other? She simply had faith.

Raised Protestant, Elizabeth's friends in Italy made a profound impact on her. Through her friends' guidance and her own study and formation, Elizabeth embraced the Catholic faith. When back home in America, she officially became Catholic. Her faith was fervent and true but extremely unpopular in her native New York, where Catholicism had just recently become legal. Undaunted, Elizabeth left for Maryland, where she would later found the American Sisters of Charity, the United States' first religious congregation of women. Elizabeth later established the first Catholic orphanage in the country and first free Catholic day school.

Maybe on those days when we feel totally done in, exhausted, and stressed, we can recall Elizabeth's faithful triumphs and know that with God's grace we can do more than we ever imagined.

I have the strength for everything through him who empowers me.
PHILIPPIANS 4:13

Saint Elizabeth Ann Seton, please pray that I, too, may accomplish with a peaceful and joyful heart all that the Lord has set before me to do.

When you are bored with life...

Saint Emilie de Rodat

Born in France in 1787, Saint Emilie is a model of service, teaching children, caring for orphans, prisoners, and the elderly. Her feast day is September 19.

When our children are finally old enough to not demand constant attention, we may find life can become a little quiet, predictable, maybe even boring. Marriages can get boring, too. After many years of togetherness, we can fall into a boring old rut. Oftentimes, boredom can lead to trouble—affairs, addictions, laziness….What can we do when life becomes predictable and dull?

Perhaps our boredom is a matter of our attitude. Saint Emilie made this point clear, explaining that she was only bored once in her life, and that was when she turned away from God and stopped practicing her faith.

Ouch! Does our complaining about boredom really mean we're turning away from God? In a way, maybe it does. After all, we each have been given our own special mission in life, and we all have countless missions laid out for us in the Bible: to preach the Gospel to the ends of the earth, to serve the poor, to love our neighbor, to pray for each other….Each is a challenge, a lifelong task. Which one or ones are we neglecting when we complain of boredom?

Learn to do good. Make justice your aim: redress the wronged, hear the orphan's plea, defend the widow.
ISAIAH 1:17

Saint Emilie, please pray that I may have the wisdom to see and the fortitude to accomplish all the missions that have been set for me.

When you need courage to stand by your decisions…

Saint Frances Cabrini

Born in Italy in 1850, Saint Frances Cabrini ended up being the first United States citizen to be canonized. With her Missionary Sisters of the Sacred Heart of Jesus, Frances founded sixty-seven hospitals, orphanages and charitable institutions. Her feast day is November 13 in the United States and December 22 in the rest of the world. She is the patron of immigrants.

In parenting, as in life, sometimes we need to heed advice, and sometimes we need to heed our own instincts. Sometimes we go around taking public opinion polls when we already know full well what the best decision is for our family. If we've discerned carefully and prayerfully, we need to stand by our decisions.

Saint Frances Cabrini traveled to New York City from her native Italy in order to work with Italian immigrants in the New World. Her first task was to open an orphanage. However, when she arrived, the archbishop advised her that plans had changed and she needed to turn around and go right back to Italy. But Frances knew what her mission was. She and her fellow sisters stayed in the U.S. and eventually founded sixty-seven institutions dedicated to the care of the poor, the unloved, the uneducated, the ill, the marginalized.

Mother Frances teaches us the importance of standing by what we know we are called to do, even when others tell us otherwise.

**Have no anxiety at all, but in everything, by prayer and petition,
with thanksgiving, make your requests known to God.
Then the peace of God that surpasses all understanding
will guard your hearts and minds in Christ Jesus.**
PHILIPPIANS 4:6–7

Saint Frances, you described the souls of those living in the Spirit as trustful with great confidence in God. As I discern God's will for my family, please pray that I may remain in the Holy Spirit, full of trust and confidence.

When someone says a hurtful remark…

Venerable Francisca del Espiritu Santo, O.P.

A native of the Philippines, Francisca lived from 1647–1711. She founded the Congregation of Dominican Sisters of Saint Catherine of Siena, Philippines. The cause for her beatification is under way.

As we prepared for the adoption of our dear baby boy, we were treated to a succession of baby showers. One such shower was given at our workplace. Afterward, a coworker asked me in my post-party euphoria, "Doesn't it feel strange to have a baby shower when you're not really expecting?" All I could manage to get out was, "Well, I am expecting a baby." I felt hurt, as if he meant that I was some type of fraud, a make-believe mom.

Afterward, I counseled myself to focus on all the joy that we experienced that day and not dwell on his comment. However, I still seethed, stewed, and treated him coolly for some time.

It seems that there are often two ways to react to hurtful comments—the stew-and-seethe way, or the, "Ah, they probably didn't mean anything by it" method. The former stirs up our anger while the latter calms us down and frees us from anger.

Sister Francisca established a new congregation which experienced some great trials. The Archbishop of Manila excommunicated Francisca at one point, but she remained prayerful and calm. When she was nearing death, Sister Francisca asked for pardon for all of her offenses against others. The priest reminded her to also pardon those who had offended her. Despite the problems she had experienced, Sister's beautiful and simple response was that no one had offended her. When I am bent on going the stew-and-seethe route, I'm turning to Sister Francisca.

> When you stand to pray, forgive anyone against whom you have a grievance, so that your heavenly Father may in turn forgive you your transgressions.
>
> MARK 11:25

Sister Francisca, at your death, you could think of no offenses committed against you. Please pray for me that I may choose to not be offended as well.

When you feel a sense of gloom...

Saint Lucy

Saint Lucy lived from 284–304 in Syracuse, Sicily. She was executed for her faith during the Diocletian persecution. Lucy is the patron of electricians and ophthalmologists, and protector from blindness and eye diseases.

Recently, I heard a coworker ask another how she was doing, to which the woman wearily responded, "The same as always: plodding along." Two minutes later, she gave the same reply to another person.

Even if we aren't quite such gray clouds, we might find that we can, on occasion, sound just as negative. How often do we appear dissatisfied, ungrateful, and negative? Probably more often than we would like to think.

As Christians, we are called to be a light to the world. We can't all be Pollyannas all the time, but our hope, peace, and joy in Christ should be obvious to those around us, and should be a source of light in a dark world.

The name Lucy means "light." Saint Lucy was an early and young Christian martyr who stood up for her faith in the midst of the darkness of persecution. Maybe we can turn to Saint Lucy for help when we feel our light dimming and our sense of gloom growing.

**Whoever follows me will not walk in darkness,
but will have the light of life.**

JOHN 8:12

Dear Saint Lucy, please pray for me that I may reflect the light of Christ in a world of shadows.

When you can't stand another houseguest...

Saint Lydia Purpuraria

"One of them, a woman named Lydia, a dealer in purple cloth, from the city of Thyatira, a worshiper of God, listened, and the Lord opened her heart to pay attention to what Paul was saying. After she and her household had been baptized, she offered us an invitation, 'If you consider me a believer in the Lord, come and stay at my home,' and she prevailed on us" (Acts 16:14–15).

It's not always easy to show hospitality. As mothers, we're already wrapped up in tending to our family's needs. Oftentimes, the last thing we want is to invite more people who need to be waited on and tended to. There are enough dishes and messes and piles of laundry created by our own brood! Guests cause us extra work and can upset the rhythms of our lives, leaving the whole household off kilter.

When we're ready to say no to sleep-overs and advise visitors to check into a hotel, we can turn to Saint Lydia, Paul's first convert in Philippi, who is famous for housing Paul and his companions in Philippi. From her home, Paul worked at establishing the first Christian community in Europe.

While it's doubtful that our guests are pursuing such a lofty goal from our living rooms, we might consider that we have established a little Christian community in our own family. Serving our guests with patience and love even when we don't feel like it allows us to model Christian values to that little Christian community. When our little ones see us smile kindly as Uncle Lester tells his favorite story for the tenth time, or they see us patiently tidying up behind their dad's old college buddy, they see Christian love in action.

Love is patient, love is kind.
1 Corinthians 13:4

Dear Saint Lydia, please pray that through hospitality to others I may show my children what Christian love looks like in the heart of our home.

When you are stressed out about homemaking tasks…

Saint Margaret Clitherow

Saint Margaret lived in England from 1556–1586. She was the first woman martyred under Queen Elizabeth's oppression of Catholics. A zealous convert to Catholicism, Margaret opened up her home to priests, which was considered treason at the time. She was imprisoned several times before her death for refusing to attend Protestant services. Her three children all entered religious life. She is remembered on October 25 as one of the forty martyrs of England and Wales.

Is Lavender Whisper or Lilac Ice the best color for the bathroom? Will the mountain of laundry ever be reduced to a hill? Will there always be an endless trail of toys and blocks weaving throughout the house?

We tend to view our homes as reflections of ourselves. Too often we can get tied up in agonizing over cleaning, decorating, and organizing.

If we consider Saint Margaret Clitherow, we may get an idea of what it really means to make a beautiful home. We don't know what her décor was like, or how tidy she was, but we do know that Mass was regularly celebrated there and priests were hidden there despite dire consequences. (Mass had been outlawed; the penalty was death for providing her home to serve as a Catholic church.)

The home is the domestic church. Saint Margaret seized the opportunity to have Mass celebrated in her home, and following her examples we can think about ways in which our home should feel like church…peaceful, prayerful, filled with Christ's love.

Like living stones, let yourselves be built into a spiritual house to be a holy priesthood….
1 PETER 2:5

Saint Margaret, you were martyred for opening your home to serve as a church. Please pray that as I go about housekeeping and homemaking tasks, I may remember that my own home truly is the domestic church.

When you are tempted to gossip…

Saint Mary Magdalene

Saint Mary Magdalene is prominent throughout all the Gospels. She was a close follower and friend of Jesus and the sister of Martha and Lazarus. Jesus had cast seven demons out of her, and she anointed him prior to the Last Supper. Mary was faithful at the foot of the cross, and she was the first recorded witness of the resurrection.

I recently heard the most scandalous bit of information about an acquaintance. It was fascinating in a horrific sense and I couldn't wait to pass it along. It was simply too intriguing to keep to myself.…Then, when I calmed down, I had to ask myself if I would be as excited to pass on good news about that same acquaintance. What if I had been told that she just completed missionary work in Haiti? Would that news burn in my mouth, looking to escape at any moment? Probably not.

When Mary Magdalene met the risen Christ outside the tomb, he told her, "Go to my brothers and tell them, 'I am going to my Father and your Father, to my God and your God." The Gospel of John explains, "Mary of Magdala went and announced to the disciples, 'I have seen the Lord!' and what he told her." The good news of Christ's resurrection was shared quickly and joyfully by this faithful disciple.

What good news can we share today? What questionable news can we keep to ourselves?

He said to them, "Go into the whole world and proclaim the gospel to every creature."
MARK 16:15

Dear Mary of Magdala, please pray that I may focus my energies on spreading the good news of Jesus and of my neighbor.

When you have to move...

Saint Mother Theodore Guerin

Born in France in 1798, Mother Theodore died in the United States in 1856. At age twenty-five, she entered the Community of Sisters of Providence. At age forty-two, she was sent to her life's work in what was then the wilderness of the New World: Indiana. She founded many schools, two orphanages, and Saint Mary of the Woods College, the first Catholic college for women in the United States. Her feast day is October 3.

Is there anything more disruptive to life than moving? As if leaving friends, loved ones, neighborhood, and home sweet home isn't hard enough, there are the exhausting tasks of packing, organizing, and unpacking into the new house. And then there's the fact that you won't be able to find your can opener, flashlight, or favorite socks for at least a month.

On top of these inconveniences and losses, we worry especially for our children—will they find friends at their new school? Will they enjoy their new home and neighborhood or long for the old?

Mother Theodore Guerin knew more than a little about uprooting. She was a sister known as a great educator in France and was making progress in rebuilding the country's educational system when she was given an altogether different mission: travel from France to what was then the Indiana territory to start a convent and a school. This involved a two-month voyage across the Atlantic, setting into the wilderness, adapting to a new culture, learning a new language, and that not-so-simple work of opening schools, orphanages, and a convent.

Surely Mother Theodore experienced a sense of loss upon leaving her home country. Surely she experienced apprehension at beginning anew in a foreign wilderness, and surely there were stumbling blocks along the way. But she had a mission and we do, too. We may not be building schools or orphanages or convents, but as mothers we are building loving homes and lives for our children, which are no small tasks.

My people will live in peaceful country, in secure dwellings and quiet resting places.
ISAIAH 32:18

Dear Mother Theodore, you know well the anxiety that accompanies beginning a new life in a new place. Please pray that I may work tirelessly and joyfully toward my mission, just as you did toward yours.

When you feel like life is not going as you planned it...

Saint Rose Philippine Duchesne

Born in France in 1769, Saint Rose entered the convent at age nineteen. At the start of the French revolution, the convent closed, and she dedicated herself to caring for the poor and sick and opened a school. At age forty-nine, she set sail to serve in the New World. She died in 1852 serving the Potawatomi Indians.

Maybe you were just about to get a promotion but had to move because your husband got transferred. Maybe you were totally ready to start a family only to be ambushed by unexpected infertility. Maybe the house you were thrilled to be buying was no longer for sale. Whatever the case, you're no stranger to life's twists and turns.

All of us ask why things can never seem to go the way we've planned. After all, we make good plans, plans that we are certain God should bless.

If anyone knows about plans gone awry, it's Saint Rose Philippine Duchesne. Desiring, planning, hoping to work with the Native Americans of Louisiana, she left her native France and sailed eleven weeks across the Atlantic Ocean. Once in the U.S., she spent seven more weeks traveling down the Mississippi River. Imagine her surprise when, upon her arrival in Louisiana, the bishop informed her that he had no place for her and her fellow sisters.

She was made to turn right back around and settle in Saint Charles, Missouri. What to do in Saint Charles? Amidst poor lodging, shortages of food, water, and money, she founded the first free school for girls west of the Mississippi. Years later, at age seventy-two, she was granted her lifelong wish to serve the Native Americans. As a missionary in Sugar Creek, Kansas, she worked with the Potawatomi, who nicknamed her "Woman-Who-Prays-Always."

Saint Rose's example teaches us how to be flexible and to adapt our plans to God's, even when it's hard.

For I know well the plans I have in mind for you—oracle of the LORD—plans for your welfare, not for woe, so as to give you a future of hope.
JEREMIAH 29:11

Saint Rose, please pray that I may follow your example of building the kingdom in whatever circumstances God places me.

CHAPTER 2

Family Life and Parenting

When you need to change your children's behavior...

Blessed Ana de los Angeles Monteagudo

A native of Peru, Blessed Ana (1604–1686) was a Dominican nun who served as novice mistress and prioress in her convent. She is venerated in her native country and by the Dominican Order on January 10.

So much of parenting is pure joy: witnessing that first smile, cuddling with an affectionate toddler, reading with a young scholar....But then, so much is a pure challenge. One of the greatest challenges is trying to change behavior that has become a habit. It could be ending pacifier dependence, reforming a constant whiner, weaning the baby off the bottle...whatever the case, at some point we reluctantly say, "This has gone too far. I have to put a stop to it."

It is so tempting to give in, to not be the "bad guy" and to just take the path of least resistance. When we reach the "give in" point, we can look to Blessed Ana de los Angeles.

Ana was appointed prioress of her scandalously lax convent and had the challenge of reforming it. This challenge involved enforcing hours of silence, confiscating the nuns' jewelry, and generally enforcing Dominican Rule. For her unpopular efforts along the way, Ana was pushed into a grave, survived poisoning attempts, and had hot coals heaped on her head. Undaunted, she continued her work until the convent was fully reformed.

Blessed Ana knew about disciplining a reluctant bunch.

Be persistent whether it is convenient or inconvenient; convince, reprimand, encourage through all patience and teaching.
2 TIMOTHY 4:2

Blessed Ana, please pray for me as I guide my little ones that I may have the patience and fortitude necessary to meet these challenging tasks.

When you need help to remain calm and gentle...

Blessed Marie-Therese Haze

Blessed Marie-Therese lived in Liege, Belgium, from 1782–1876. She founded the Congregation of the Daughters of the Cross of Liege to educate poor children, but her mission eventually expanded to include nursing the sick, ministering to prisoners, and sheltering the poor. She is venerated on the date of her death, January 7.

None of us wants to be the harsh, loud, short-tempered mom. But, of course, there are days when we may feel like that description fits us a little too well. We get tired after being up half the night with our baby, we get frustrated asking a little one to pick up his toys, we get aggravated with our teenager's eye rolling, and pretty soon, there we are: harsh, loud, short-tempered.

Is it possible to remain a calm presence in our home (most of the time)? Blessed Marie-Therese Haze of Belgium would convince us that we could. Although she did not have children to care for, she spent her life serving others who challenged her patience and fortitude greatly. Blessed Marie-Therese spent much of her life serving prisoners and then founded a shelter for prostitutes and street women. Surely she had trying moments and days serving the outcasts of society. However, she was remembered as calm, treating all people with dignity, even when reprimanding them.

As mothers, we seek to correct our children's misbehavior and teach them virtuous behavior. Let's pray that we can do that calmly and while recognizing each child's dignity.

She opens her mouth in wisdom; kindly instruction is on her tongue.
PROVERBS 31:26

Blessed Marie-Therese, please pray that I may correct and guide my children gently and wisely, especially on those most trying days.

When you have a suffering child...

Blessed Mother—the Crucifixion

"Standing by the cross of Jesus were his mother and his mother's sister..." (John 19:25).

There may be nothing more heartbreaking than a sick baby. Whether it's an ear infection or a stomach virus, we feel our children's pain and a terrible sense of helplessness. At such times, I think of mothers of children who truly suffer with serious illnesses, injuries, or hunger. To whom do we turn for prayers and for a role model when our children are in real pain? The Blessed Mother.

As we struggle to see our children through their most difficult hours and days, we can turn to the one who walked with her suffering son on the road to Calvary. When that little fevered head rests fitfully on our chest, we can turn to the one who saw her son's precious head crowned in thorns. When we have to hold a frightened child by the hand, we can turn to the one who witnessed her child's hands nailed to a cross.

She knows our pain, and her powerful prayers can help us bear it.

"Whoever wishes to come after me must deny himself, take up his cross, and follow me. For whoever wishes to save his life will lose it, but whoever loses his life for my sake will find it.
MATTHEW 16:24–25

Holy Mary, Mother of God, you stood by your son as he endured horrific suffering. Please pray that I may have the strength to help my children carry their crosses of suffering.

When you fear you're failing in your role as a mother…

Blessed Mother—Finding in the Temple

"When his parents saw him, they were astonished, and his mother said to him, 'Son, why have you done this to us? Your father and I have been looking for you with great anxiety.' And he said to them, 'Why were you looking for me? Did you not know that I must be in my Father's house?' But they did not understand what he said to them. He went down with them and came to Nazareth, and was obedient to them" (Luke 2:48–51).

All of us have had moments, days, weeks, maybe even years when we feel that we are failures as mothers. Maybe we're afraid that we let the baby cry in her crib too long, or we were short of patience with a fussy youngster, or we haven't spent enough time with each child.

Whatever the specifics, we chastise ourselves, asking, "How could I? What kind of a mother…."

The Blessed Mother knows something about this feeling. She was chosen by God to bear and raise his only begotten Son. She knew that her sole purpose in life was to raise this child. Imagine the weight of this responsibility! Imagine her feeling when she realized that this most precious son was missing. Not missing for an hour or two, but for three days as she and Joseph searched frantically among crowds of travelers. Surely she asked herself, "How could I? What kind of a mother…."

Happily, Jesus is finally found preaching in the temple. How did the Holy Family recover from this episode? Nowhere does Scripture imply that their relationship was damaged for all eternity. In fact, according to Luke, Jesus "advanced in wisdom and age and favor before God and man." Something tells me our children will do likewise in spite of our failings along the way.

And his mother kept all these things in her heart.
LUKE 2:51

Holy Mary, Mother of God, you know all the anxieties of motherhood. Please pray that I may have peace knowing that God will take care of my family.

When you feel anxiety over an upcoming birth or adoption…

Blessed Mother—the Nativity of our Lord

"While they were there, the time came for her to have her child, and she gave birth to her firstborn son. She wrapped him in swaddling clothes and laid him in a manger, because there was no room for them in the inn" (Luke 2:6–7).

Anticipating the arrival of a child should be a joyful time. So many dreams, so much excitement go into those months leading up to the big day. And yet, childbirth can be a frightening prospect. Every other mother we meet is happy to share with us the details of her difficult, painful, and long labor and delivery. And the birthing books meant to prepare women can be nerve-wracking as well, as there are always large sections devoted to every possible complication.

Adoptive moms are spared the worry of physical pain, but we brace ourselves for any number of possible challenges. The adoption books warn us of the perils of Reactive Attachment Disorder. We wonder, "Will this child attach to me? Will he grieve terribly for the foster family/orphanage?" And on and on.

The Blessed Mother has some experience with welcoming a new baby into the world. Most experts agree that Mary was likely a young teenager when she gave birth to baby Jesus. And though she was sinless, she surely wasn't without anxiety at the time of his birth. Undoubtedly, she would have liked to have given birth surrounded by the mature women of her family, confident and experienced in the birthing process. But such was not the case, as she found herself in a cold stable, surrounded by animals with only dear Saint Joseph to help her.

Yet, it was enough: Baby Jesus was born, and from that point on, the miracles never stopped. God provided for the Holy Family, just as he will provide for yours.

When cares increase within me, your comfort gives me joy.
PSALM 94:19

Holy Mary, Mother of God, please pray for me that I may be filled with joy and peace as I await the arrival of my child.

When you seek to be the "perfect" mom...

Blessed Teresa of Calcutta

Agnes Bojaxhiu, now known worldwide as "Mother Teresa," was born in Macedonia in 1910. A Sister of Loreto, she was sent to India, where she spent years educating wealthy girls. Teresa began to experience a series of visions in which Jesus asked her to serve the poorest of the poor. She did just that for the rest of her life, founding the Missionaries of Charity.

When I have visited a friend whose house is spotless and whose life seems perfectly organized, I feel more than a twinge of inferiority. I'm forever behind on everything that needs to be done, and our house looks like a toy factory merged with a laundromat that then blew up.

Why can't I keep up? I wonder. I want to be the organized, efficient, got-it-together mom. I want my son to have a household that runs like a machine, with a mom who juggles everything calmly and expertly.

Blessed Teresa of Calcutta has insight to share with those of us seeking after perfection. She once said that we are not all called to do great things, but we are called to do little things with great love. Not with great efficiency, not even with great skill. Great love.

Blessed Teresa should help us realize that when our children grow up, we want more than anything for them to remember feeling happy and loved from the little things. A mom who made time to play in the sandbox, to dance in the kitchen, and to read to them in bed. We want them to recall a mom who did these littlest things with the greatest love.

So faith, hope, love remain, these three; but the greatest of these is love.
1 Corinthians 13:13

Blessed Teresa, thank you for reminding us that we are first called to be loving. Please pray that I may perform all my tasks, however small, with great love.

When you want to give God thanks for your children...

Saint Hannah

Hannah is one of the many women of the Bible who struggled with infertility. Eventually, after much prayer and weeping, she is given the child Samuel, whom she offers back to God completely. She later had two daughters and three more sons. Her feast day is December 9, and she is the patron of poverty and childless people.

Surely we all view our children as our most precious gifts from God. Especially if we have had trouble conceiving, we are overwhelmed with joy at the positive pregnancy test/successful adoption. We rejoice at every milestone great and small thereafter. We are thankful for their health, their love, and all their darling little ways.

Hannah, mother of Samuel, went beyond telling God that she was grateful for the child she conceived after years of infertility. Once she weaned Samuel, she literally gave him back to the Lord by sending him to live forever in the temple with the priest, Eli.

Surely no one would suggest that we leave our toddlers at the neighborhood parish, but the act of giving our children back to the Lord is one to emulate. We can use the words Hannah spoke as she took Samuel to the temple: "As long as he lives, he shall be dedicated to the LORD." We can pray for our children, asking God to keep them holy and to help them find their path. We can explain to them that their life was a gift from God, and we know they will make it a gift right back to him.

**I prayed for this child and the LORD granted my request.
Now I, in turn, give him to the LORD.**
1 SAMUEL 1:27–28

Dear Saint Hannah, please pray that I may be ever mindful of the fact that my children are precious gifts from the Lord.

When you introduce devotional practices to your family...

Saint Margaret Mary Alacoque

Born in France in 1647, Saint Margaret Mary is known for spreading devotion to the Sacred Heart of Jesus. This devotion was officially recognized by Pope Clement XIII in 1765. She is the patron of devotees of the Sacred Heart, polio patients, and those who have lost their parents.

As Catholic moms, it is likely that we all have certain devotions we would like to promote in our family. Maybe it is saying the rosary or a novena together, going to reconciliation regularly as a family, or perhaps something as simple as saying grace together before meals. Unfortunately, it is also likely that our devotion is not enthusiastically greeted by each family member. We may meet with eye rolling, complaints, or even outright refusals.

What to do? Call on Saint Margaret Mary Alacoque. You're probably familiar with the image of Christ's Sacred Heart—a heart inflamed and wrapped in a crown of thorns, and you may be familiar with "first Friday" devotions to the Sacred Heart. Both the image and the devotional practices were revealed by Christ to Saint Margaret Mary when she was a young nun.

Just as we may meet with opposition to our devotional practices, Margaret Mary was scolded harshly by her superior for daring to claim that Jesus made these revelations to her. In time, the truth of her revelations was recognized, and devotion to the Sacred Heart has spread like the fire in the image itself. Perhaps our family devotional practices will spread in the same way.

Come, let us sing joyfully to the LORD;
cry out to the rock of our salvation.
PSALM 95:1

When you need to teach your children charity...

Saint Margaret of Scotland

Saint Margaret was born in Hungary in 1045, and married Malcolm, king of Scotland. The couple had eight children. She was educated and faithful, and a great influence on her husband and the country he ruled. Margaret is the patron of large families, queens, widows, and those who have lost children. Her feast day is November 16.

Surely we all want the best for our children. We want them to have a nice home, good schools, a safe neighborhood, and on and on. Is it possible, though, that in our quest to provide our children with the good life, we actually provide them with a life that is totally insulated from all the suffering of the world? Perhaps when Scripture speaks of tending to the poor and the outcast, they cannot picture who this might be and have no way to comprehend that there is a world in need outside their front door.

Saint Margaret, queen of Scotland, could easily have insulated herself and her royal family from the needy of her time. However, she took seriously the Lord's direction to care for the poor. She personally washed their feet and never sat down to eat without first feeding orphans and impoverished adults.

Margaret has much to teach us about serving the poor—and about teaching our children, by example, to do so as well.

> For I was hungry and you gave me food, I was thirsty and you
> gave me drink, a stranger and you welcomed me, naked and you
> clothed me, ill and you cared for me, in prison and you visited me.
>
> MATTHEW 25:35–36

Saint Margaret, you were a model of Christian charity for your children. Please pray that I may follow your example of service and share my love for the needy with my children.

When you struggle to forgive those who hurt your child...

Saint Maria Goretti

A native of Italy, Maria Goretti lived only twelve years (1890–1902). Her life was cut short by an attacker who stabbed her to death. Maria is well-known for the forgiveness she offered her killer on her deathbed. She is the patron of girls, rape victims, martyrs, and those who have lost their parents. Her feast day is July 6.

It is delightful to experience our children's innocence. No one has ever been unkind to them, so everyone in the world is their friend. We know that it will be heartbreaking when that first bully hurts his little feelings. Perhaps it will not only be heartbreaking, but also anger-inducing.

It's inevitable that other children will be unkind to ours, and probably just as inevitable that a teacher, coach, employer, or other adult will treat them harshly and unfairly at some point. Is it possible for protective mamas to forgive these individuals?

Twelve-year-old Maria Goretti was stabbed to death by a would-be rapist. While dying in the hospital, she proclaimed her wholehearted forgiveness for her killer, Alessandro. Years later, Alessandro approached Maria's mother for forgiveness. Knowing that her daughter had forgiven this man, Maria's mother was able to do so as well. In time, he attended Maria's canonization ceremony with her family.

Each of us has an undying devotion to our children and would protect them from all harm if only we could. But we are called to forgive those who hurt them, even as we do our best to protect them. And sometimes we are called to emulate even our own children's freely given forgiveness.

> **But I say to you, love your enemies, and pray for those
> who persecute you, that you may be children of your heavenly Father,
> for he makes his sun rise on the bad and the good, and causes rain
> to fall on the just and the unjust.**
> MATTHEW 5:44–45

Saint Maria, your deathbed forgiveness of Alessandro must surely have helped your mother find forgiveness in her heart. Please pray for me when I struggle with forgiving those who hurt my dear children.

When you are worried about your wayward child...

Saint Monica

Saint Monica lived in Algeria from 331–387. She was the mother of the famous Saint Augustine, bishop and Doctor of the Church. Saint Monica's feast day is August 27, and she is the patron of wives and abuse victims.

Moms usually have the role of Chief Family Coaxer. When children are very young, we coax them into putting on their jammies, picking up their blocks, and taking one more bite of their dinner. Later, we coax them into doing their homework, practicing their instruments, and writing thank-you notes.

But what about when our children turn into young adults who lose their faith or lose interest in their faith? It's disheartening, upsetting, and worrisome. Should we coax them into going to church? Can a mom cajole a child into an active faith life? Must we nag them into praying? Can we argue them into the sacraments? No.

What we can do is look to Saint Monica as our role model. She prayed diligently for her difficult husband and mother-in-law until they converted from paganism to Catholicism. When her son, Augustine, resisted converting to the Christian faith, she prayed. And she prayed. Then she prayed some more. For seventeen years she prayed for this wayward child. When she wasn't praying herself, she reached out for help and asked priests to pray for her son, too. (Some sources say that local priests started to duck away when they saw Monica coming.)

Eventually, she befriended Saint Ambrose, whose preaching was instrumental in her son's conversion. Shortly before her death, Saint Monica witnessed Saint Ambrose baptize this wayward son. From heaven, she watched as this same son became a bishop, great theologian, and Doctor of the Church.

Saint Monica's constant prayers for a son she knew was far from God can inspire us in our own prayerful parenting. Though we may never see our children turn down the path we hope for them, we can know that God hears our prayers.

Whatever you ask for in prayer with faith, you will receive.
MATTHEW 21:22

Dear Saint Monica, you know what it means to have a wayward child. Please pray that I may be constant and faithful in prayer for my own child. Please also pray for my child, that he/she may return to the Faith.

When you are preparing your children for their sacraments...

Servant of God Carolina Bellandi Palladini

Born in Italy in 1895, Carolina and her husband never had children, but she found a unique way to serve the children of her community. In her later years, although she herself had no money, she worked to financially support cloistered nuns. The cause for her canonization began on October 18, 2001.

If you are teaching religious education classes or just trying mightily to instruct your own children in the Faith, it is easy to dismiss your role and ministry as minor. It's just a few kids, you may tell yourself, just a couple hours a week....

When we begin to think that our work with teaching the Faith to little ones is no big deal, consider that the Church is seeking to canonize Carolina, whose ministry was to help children celebrate their very first Eucharist.

Carolina Bellandi Palladini had no children of her own but devoted herself to young first communicants. Carolina and her followers arranged for the children to be instructed and prepared for the sacrament by area priests. They also provided appropriate clothing for each child and a celebratory reception afterward. Over the years, it is estimated that Carolina helped twenty thousand youngsters celebrate their first communion. Carolina had no money herself but always obtained sufficient donations from what she called the bank of Jesus.

Reflecting on Carolina's labor of love can teach us how we should approach preparing our own children for the sacraments: with care and concern, and trust that God will provide what is needed. The time we spend on this most important endeavor can lead to lifelong faith.

**Train the young in the way they should go; even when old,
they will not swerve from it.**

PROVERBS 22:6

When you struggle in your marriage…

Blessed Elisabetta Canori Mora

Blessed Elisabetta lived in Rome from 1774–1825, and was a wife, mother, and member of the Trinitarian Third Order. She is known for her constant prayers for the conversion of her wayward husband, who had an affair and abandoned his family.

There is no way to live with any person and avoid all conflict indefinitely. Our marriage relationship is no exception. I recall an interview with Billy Graham's wife, Ruth. She was asked if she had ever, in the course of her long marriage, considered divorce. She replied that no, she hadn't, but she had indeed considered murder. Like all of us, she loved her dear husband, but there were challenging times.

We can deal with these challenging periods in any number of ways: we can seek advice from friends or therapists, read self-help books, and attend marriage workshops. For some reason, though, praying for our husbands and our marriage is not always the first remedy that comes to mind. Sometimes we're so angry or hurt that praying for him is the last thing we want to do, even though it would be the most efficacious.

Blessed Elisabetta constantly prayed for her unfaithful and unloving husband. Even as she and her daughters suffered emotionally and financially because of his actions, she saw it as her task to offer up her suffering and pray for his change of heart. After Elisabetta's death, he repented and eventually became a priest.

Elisabetta's example of constant prayer for her husband is one we can all follow in our marriages, both in good times and in bad.

> [I have not stopped] giving thanks for you,
> remembering you in my prayers.
> EPHESIANS 1:16

Blessed Elisabetta, please pray that I may be in constant prayer for the good of my husband, our marriage, and our family.

When you need to help mend broken relationships...

Saint Catherine of Siena

Saint Catherine of Siena lived in Italy from 1347–1380, and belonged to the Third Order of Saint Dominic. Catherine was influential in trying to bring about peace and justice in this chaotic period of Church history. She was named a Doctor of the Church, and along with Edith Stein and Bridget of Sweden, is the patron of Europe. Her feast day is April 29.

Quarrels, spats, disputes, misunderstandings. All families have had their share of each. Maybe we have grown children who are not on speaking terms. Or maybe there is a rift between our own siblings. Whatever the case, sometimes we tell ourselves that we don't want to meddle, don't want to get in the middle of things. It's easy to convince ourselves that we're right not to "interfere." But, what if a kind word or a bit of encouragement could make the difference and help to end a conflict?

Saint Catherine of Siena, often described as one of the most brilliant women in history, was probably tempted to just mind her own business and not interfere in the great conflicts of her day. But interfere, or more appropriately, intervene, she did.

Though a young nun with no formal education, Catherine was amazingly influential in resolving the conflicts of her time. When Pope Gregory XI prohibited the city of Florence from receiving the sacraments, the people sent Catherine as their ambassador to the Pope. Later, she convinced Pope Gregory to return the papacy to Rome from Avignon. In the last years of her short life, she was summoned by Pope Urban VI to help end the Western Schism. (Unfortunately, at the time of her death it was still yet to be resolved.)

Maybe when we see conflict, bitterness, and division in our midst, we can call on this peacemaker to pray for us.

Blessed are the peacemakers, for they will be called children of God.
MATTHEW 5:9

Saint Catherine, you are a model for all who wish to bring about reconciliation. Please pray that I may respond with wisdom and gentleness to help end conflicts in my own family.

When you seek a closer relationship with family…

Saint Scholastica

The twin sister of Saint Benedict, Saint Scholastica is one of our earlier saints, living from 480–543. She is the patron of convulsive children, nuns, and against rain. Her feast day is February 10.

Most every family tree has some cracks, some weak points, and even some broken branches caused by bitterness, anger, and resentment. Sometimes it's easiest to just give up on restoring relationships. We're busy with our own children, we tell ourselves, and don't have the energy to worry about brother/sister/cousin so-and-so. Or maybe our children are older and we've had a terrible falling out with one of them. We may be tempted to let hurt feelings fester there, too.

Saint Scholastica's life shows us that God answers those who pray for familial closeness. Saint Scholastica's twin brother was Saint Benedict.

He founded a monastery, and she entered a convent. Benedict's Rule permitted them to see each other just once a year. They would meet to visit each other at a small cabin near the monastery.

As Benedict prepared to depart the evening of their yearly visit, Scholastica begged him to stay. He refused, so she turned to God and prayed fervently. Immediately, an intense storm erupted, prohibiting Benedict from leaving. For just a little while longer, Scholastica would get to enjoy the company of her dear brother. Some day, perhaps we'll get to do the same with a loved one.

For the sake of my brothers and friends I say, "Peace be with you."
PSALM 122:8

Saint Scholastica, when your brother turned to leave, you prayed to the Lord that he would stay. Please pray that when my loved ones turn from me, I may turn to God in faith.

CHAPTER 3

Following God's Call

When you contemplate your ultimate goal as a mother...

Saint Anne, Mother of Mary

Tradition tells us that Anne and Joachim were the parents of the Blessed Mother. She and Joachim are the patrons of married couples, and she is also the patron of horsewomen, woodworkers, and antique dealers. Her feast day is July 26.

As Catholics, we believe that Mary was conceived without sin, set apart as holy even before her birth. This means that her mother, Saint Anne, was given the responsibility and honor of bearing this sinless child, of raising this holy daughter who would in time bear and raise the Savior.

Saint Anne makes us consider that all of us moms have been given a great responsibility and honor. No, we're not raising the Mother of God, as Saint Anne did, but we have no clue as to how God wants to use our children for his glory. We may have been entrusted to raise future missionaries, priests, nuns, teachers of the Faith, or martyrs. We don't know exactly what they are to become, but we know our job is to keep them holy, faithful, and to model Christian love for them.

It's a daunting task, one Saint Anne would be happy to pray for.

Mary said, "Behold, I am the handmaid of the Lord.
May it be done to me according to your word."
LUKE 1:38

Saint Anne, you had the awesome privilege and responsibility of raising the Mother of God. I humbly ask for your powerful intercession as I try to raise holy, faithful children ready to answer God's call.

When you feel repentant...

Saint Teresa of Avila

A Doctor of the Church, Saint Teresa is one of the most well-known and beloved of all women saints. She lived in Spain in the sixteenth century as a Carmelite nun. Her spiritual journey is described in her books Autobiography, The Interior Castle, *and* The Way to Perfection. *She is the patron of those ridiculed for their faith, in religious orders, suffering from headaches, lace makers, and those who have lost their parents. Her feast day is October 15.*

"How could I have done that?"

"Why did I ever say such a thing?"

"When will I ever learn my lesson?"

Do any of these sound familiar? Although extreme penances and acts of self-mortification are no longer popular practices among the faithful, we sure do like to beat ourselves up in this modern age.

Saint Teresa of Avila lived in the sixteenth century, a time when extreme penance and austerity were standard practice. However, in her straightforward, simple, understandable way, she explained exactly what people should do after they have done something wrong. Given the time period, we might suspect that she would recommend any number of rigorous penances. But she didn't. If one does something wrong, she advised, he should change.

Simple yet profound advice! Can we follow it? If we snap at our children and husband, if we gossip, if we're lazy, if we're dishonest, whatever our vice, we need not beat ourselves up and rehash our errors in our mind. We can seek and gain God's forgiveness, and then, as Saint Teresa advised—change!

> **Cast away from you all the crimes you have committed,**
> **and make for yourselves a new heart and a new spirit.**
> EZEKIEL 18:31

Saint Teresa of Avila, thank you for your good advice! Please pray that I may look forward and not dwell on my past mistakes.

When you are filled with joy and gratitude...

Blessed Mother—the Magnificat

"My soul proclaims the greatness of the Lord; my spirit rejoices in God my savior" (Luke 1:46–47).

We all have times of joy that lead us to praise and thank God for the gifts we've been given that are impossible to ignore.

I remember excitedly preparing for our first Christmas with our baby boy. I was decorating the Christmas tree as my husband and the baby played nearby. Snow was falling outside, a rare December treat for central Kentucky. It was so peaceful and so lovely, the fulfillment of so many dreams and prayers.

What words can we use to express our gratitude for times of peace and joy? Try Mary's Magnificat, also called "Canticle of Mary" in the Gospel of Luke. The Blessed Mother prayed these words not long after agreeing to be the mother of Jesus.

We often think of the sorrows of the Blessed Mother, but I like pondering these words she used when she experienced great joy, too. We can use these words ourselves when we want to express our gratitude for all our joyful moments, answered prayers, whenever we rejoice in the many blessings of God our Savior.

The Mighty One has done great things for me, and holy is his name.
LUKE 1:49

Holy Mary, Mother of God, thank you for these joyful words. Please pray that I may always imitate you and give thanks to God for all the joy in my life.

When you want to show God your gratitude...

Peter's Mother-in-Law

Saint Peter's mother-in-law is mentioned briefly in the Gospel of Matthew as one of the many people whom Jesus heals.

Since becoming a mother, "Lord, please..." is always on my lips. As soon as I finish one request, I am on to another.

If you're like me, you're probably spending a lot of time asking God for things in prayer. "Lord, please calm this baby's fears," I remember praying over and over as I held my very frightened nine-month-old baby the day we adopted him. "Lord, please let him love us...." Sometimes amid all our requests, we forget to pause and thank God for what we've been given.

All we know about Peter's mother-in-law is that she was ill with a fever, Jesus quickly cured her, and "she rose and waited on him" (Matthew 8:15). It's this "rose and waited on" or "served" him that might give us pause.

When our prayers are answered, in the busyness of life, we may say a quick prayer of thanks and scramble on. Maybe we can remember Peter's mother-in-law and recognize our daily miracles, rise and serve him in thanksgiving.

I am grateful to him who has strengthened me, Christ Jesus our Lord, because he considered me trustworthy in appointing me to the ministry.
1 TIMOTHY 1:12

Dear Mother-in-Law of Peter, Scripture tells us that when Jesus healed you, you immediately stood and waited on him. Please pray that I may follow your example and express my thanks by service to the Lord.

When you need to take action...

Saint Katharine Drexel

Born in Philadelphia in 1858, Saint Katharine grew up in a prestigious, wealthy family with a strong social conscience. She eventually founded the order known today as the Sisters of the Blessed Sacrament and devoted her life to the service of African Americans and Native Americans, for whom she established more than fifty schools. The most famous of these is Xavier University of Louisiana in New Orleans. Her feast day is March 3.

"Someone should really help…"

"Why doesn't anyone organize…"

Sometimes it is just so obvious that something needs to be done in our community, parish, our children's schools, our workplace, and the world at large.

Saint Katharine Drexel, a young woman from a wealthy family, gained an audience with Pope Leo XIII. She wanted to speak to him about sending missionaries to the United States to help the Native Americans and former slaves. To her request, the Pope suggested that she herself become a missionary. And so she did, and dedicated the rest of her life to service to African Americans and Native Americans.

Maybe there is one cause, one project, that doesn't need someone, but actually needs me.

My sheep hear my voice; I know them, and they follow me.
JOHN 10:27

Saint Katharine, you saw a need and devoted your life to filling it. Please pray that I may discern what the Lord's special mission is for me.

When you need assistance in answering God's call…

Blessed Mother—the Visitation

"During those days, Mary set out and traveled to the hill country in haste to a town of Judah, where she entered the house of Zechariah and greeted Elizabeth" (Luke 1:39–40).

"In haste." Mary receives the biggest news anyone can receive. She knows her role, her mission, her life's plan, and she goes in haste to share this with Elizabeth.

What does this mean for us? Maybe when our mission is clear, we need to quickly strengthen ourselves with the company of fellow believers. Whatever we're to do, whether we're called to begin a Bible study, become a foster parent, or go on a mission trip, we need to seek out others who can encourage and assist us on our mission. And we need to do it quickly.

When Mary reaches her cousin, Elizabeth immediately celebrates and encourages Mary with her words, "Most blessed are you among women, and blessed is the fruit of your womb!" We, too, are called to celebrate God's great plan with others who will support and encourage us to follow it.

Therefore, encourage one another and build one another up, as indeed you do.
1 THESSALONIANS 5:11

Dear Mary, Mother of God, please pray that I may seek and find trusted, faithful friends to support and encourage me in the work God has for me. Please pray that I may also support and encourage others in their missions.

When you feel called to serve the least among us...

Blessed Mother Mary of Saint Joseph
(Laura Evangelista)

Born in Venezuela in 1875, Mother Mary cofounded the Augustinian Recollects of the Heart of Jesus. Hers was a life of service; she founded thirty-seven homes for the elderly and orphans. She died at the age of ninety-two.

Motherhood is all about caregiving.

We know that caring for any child is a wonderful, challenging, and rewarding vocation. Sometimes, looking into our baby's eyes and knowing that there are so many babies who will never have anyone to hold and love them makes us desire to care for still more children, or for others in need in the world. We consider becoming foster mothers, adoptive mothers, or volunteers in orphanages.

When we're discerning what role we might take in caring for the least among us, we might ask for the prayers of Blessed Laura Evangelista. She and Father Vincente Lopez Aveledo founded a congregation dedicated to nursing the sick poor, or as she described them, those who were rejected by all and wanted by none.

Mother Mary of Saint Joseph can help us become sensitive to the fact that all the marginalized, impoverished sick of the world were once somebody's babies, and the world has become a cold and cruel place for them. If you feel God calling you to a life of caring for the least among us, seek Blessed Laura's intercession.

> **The just care for the cause of the poor; the wicked do not understand such care.**
> **PROVERBS 29:7**

Dear Blessed Laura, my mission, like yours, is to serve the vulnerable of the world. Please pray that I may have the strength, patience, and love to carry out this mission.

When you think God's call doesn't make sense...

Saint Bernadette

Saint Bernadette Soubirous was a native of France and lived from 1844–1879. She grew up in a desperately poor family in the little town of Lourdes, and out of the blue, while running an errand, she was visited by the Blessed

We all know that we're supposed to respond in obedience when God calls us. But have you ever felt that God was asking you to do something outside the realm of possibility or reason or just beyond your capabilities? Maybe you feel called to lead a Bible study even though you're scared to death of public speaking. Maybe he is leading you to leave your perfectly safe career for something more challenging and fulfilling. Maybe he's planned for you to adopt an unknown child on the other side of the world.

"I couldn't possibly do that!" you may want to respond. "It's too difficult, too scary; it's just out of the question."

Saint Bernadette Soubirous, now famous for the Marian apparitions that she experienced in Lourdes, France, knows a little bit about being called to do things outside the realm of possibility.

The ninth time that the Blessed Mother appeared to her, she instructed Bernadette, "Go drink at the spring and wash in it." The only problem was that there was no spring where the Blessed Mother beckoned. Even so, Bernadette sought to obey. She scratched at the ground and brought up first mud, and then muddy water. She endeavored to wash with the muddy water, to the horror of the crowd gathered around the grotto. Their horror turned to amazement when they later discovered a spring bubbling up in the exact place where Bernadette scratched the earth. Over time, millions of people have bathed in the spring believed to have healing powers.

Bernadette's humble obedience to a call she did not understand can teach us to find the courage to carry out God's will for our lives, even if it doesn't seem to make sense.

I have the strength for everything through him who empowers me.
PHILIPPIANS 4:13

Saint Bernadette, I believe that God is calling me to a great challenge. Please pray that I may respond in faith and obedience.

When you want to hear and answer God's call...

Saint Joan of Arc

Born in 1412 in France, Joan heard heavenly messages from a young age, instructing her to help the king of France regain the throne. Eventually she was given a small army, which she led to victory. Later captured, Joan found herself in the cross hairs of a complicated conflict of church and state. She was brought before a tribunal and accused and convicted of heresy and sorcery. Burned at the stake for her crimes, Joan was later exonerated of all guilt. She is the patron of France, and her feast day is May 30.

She didn't even know how to ride a horse, and she certainly didn't know how to fight a war, but Saint Joan of Arc did know how to listen. She heard the voices of angels and saints from ages thirteen to sixteen. At fourteen, the voices told her to save France from the English. The voice of Saint Michael the Archangel told her that this command came straight from God.

Joan could have listed a thousand and one reasons to disobey the command, but she didn't. Instead, as outlandish as they seemed, she accepted her orders and went on to achieve amazing victories for her country.

Most of us don't hear God's messengers whispering in our ears. Most of us won't be called to save our country through miraculous feats of warfare. But all of us can increase our awareness of God's call.

Sometimes he speaks to our current situation through Scripture, sometimes through extraordinary circumstances, sometimes through the words of a fellow believer, and once in a while almost as directly and clearly as he spoke to Joan. How is he speaking to us today? Are we listening?

Oh, that today you would hear his voice: Do not harden your hearts.
PSALM 95:7–8

Saint Joan of Arc, you are a model of listening to and obeying God's call. Please pray that I may learn to listen to his voice today.

CHAPTER 4

Faith Struggles

When you lack a devotion to Mary...

Saint Elizabeth

Cousin of Mary and wife of Zechariah, Saint Elizabeth was another of the once-barren women of the Bible. Mary runs to her immediately after learning that she is to be the mother of Jesus and that Elizabeth has conceived a son in her old age. Her feast day is November 5, and she is the patron saint of pregnant women.

"Hail Mary, full of grace...." The words of this prayer are so familiar that we may have long ago stopped thinking about what they mean. The same may be said for rosaries and other Marian devotions. Ho hum, let's say the rosary. Hope it doesn't take too long. Oh, it's a Marian feast day, guess we'll go to Mass if we have time.

If you've lost or never had a devotion to Mary, consider Saint Elizabeth. Mary went "in haste" to see Elizabeth shortly after learning that she would be the mother of the Savior. Upon greeting Mary, Elizabeth wonders aloud, "How does this happen to me, that the mother of my Lord should come to me" (Luke 1:43)?

This exclamation of amazement sums up the feeling we should have when we pray a Hail Mary or call upon the Blessed Mother's intercession. How does this happen that the Mother of the Lord should come to us? How does it happen that she who raised the Savior could now pray for us as we raise our children?

May we always have Saint Elizabeth's sense of wonder at the miracle of Mary's presence in our lives.

> **And Elizabeth, filled with the holy Spirit, cried out in a loud voice and said, "Most blessed are you among women, and blessed is the fruit of your womb."**
>
> LUKE 1:41–42

Dear Saint Elizabeth, thank you for filling me with awe at the realization that I can call upon the intercession of the Mother of God. Please pray that I always keep this devotion to Mary.

When you need to feel and share God's mercy...

Saint Faustina Kowalska

A native of Poland, Saint Faustina lived from 1905–1938. By all appearances, she lived a very simple life as a nun. However, after her death, her now famous diary Divine Mercy in My Soul *was discovered. In it, she recorded the words Christ spoke to her. He also revealed an image of himself to Saint Faustina. This image, bearing the phrase, "Jesus, I trust in you," is growing in popularity in churches and homes.*

We often hear that the hardest person to forgive is yourself. Most of us have incidents, decisions, and mistakes for which we may believe we could never forgive ourselves. Even after going to confession and knowing in our minds that God forgives us, in our hearts, we can still hang on to regret, frustration, and guilt.

One might wonder if this difficulty in forgiving ourselves may affect our ability to forgive others. We may subconsciously think, "If I haven't forgiven myself for what I did years ago, do you really think I'll forgive you for what you did yesterday?" Indeed, how can we show mercy to others if we do not accept God's gift of mercy for ourselves?

Saint Faustina's special mission was to make known Christ's great mercy. She is famous for the revelations Christ gave to her personally, all focused on his mercy. She prayed, "O my Jesus, each of your saints reflects one of your virtues. I desire to reflect your compassionate heart, full of mercy" (*Diary* 1242). What a beautiful prayer! May it become ours today.

> **When you stand to pray, forgive anyone against whom you have a grievance, so that your heavenly Father may in turn forgive you your transgressions.**
> MARK 11:25

Dear Saint Faustina, please pray that I may reflect Jesus' mercy to both myself and to those around me.

When you are tempted to be prideful...

Saint Hyacintha Mariscotti

Saint Hyacintha was born into a noble family in Italy in 1588. She caused such trouble for her family that they virtually forced her into the convent. Once there, she continued to live as nobility but had an abrupt and profound change of heart and lived the rest of her days as a model Franciscan sister. Her feast day is January 30.

Somewhere along the line, we may have gotten the idea that we are above reproach. A friend expresses surprise at our propensity for gossip, and we get defensive. Our mother asks us about something we said to our children, and we tense up. Our boss tells us to try to get along better with a fellow employee, and we immediately balk. "Who is this person to tell me how to act?" we ask. "Does she think she's so perfect?"

When our pride gets in the way of our better judgment, we can consider Saint Hyacintha. This saint came from a wealthy family and kept up her comfortable lifestyle even after entering the convent. Upon visiting her during an illness, Hyacintha's confessor expressed his surprise at her comparatively lavish quarters and suggested that she live more humbly. Instead of reacting angrily or dismissively, Hyacintha began to undergo a metamorphosis. She substantively changed her lifestyle and developed a special devotion to the sufferings of Christ.

What if we took a cue from Saint Hyacintha? Could we not also set aside our pride and carefully consider the suggestions or (ouch!) the criticisms of others?

When pride comes, disgrace comes; but with the humble is wisdom.
PROVERBS 11:2

Saint Hyacintha, I am so easily offended. Please pray that I may hear the truth that others bring to me and respond in wisdom and humility.

When you lack a focus on Christ...

Saint Martha

Saint Martha was a special friend of Jesus and the sister of Mary and Lazarus. Jesus visited their home, and she grew impatient with her sister, Mary, who sat at Jesus' feet while she was busy with hostess duties. Martha is the patron of cooks, and her feast day is July 29.

Many of us are familiar with the story of Mary and Martha. Mary sat and listened attentively to Jesus, and Martha was serving, angry that Mary wasn't helping. It can seem so unfair that Mary was praised while Martha, the worker bee, was reprimanded by Jesus.

As moms, we understand Martha more than Mary—we're usually on our feet, tending to everybody's needs until we get irritable. Who could blame Martha for getting a little testy?

But Mary teaches us that nothing should have been more important than Jesus. Martha should have realized this. You don't let God Incarnate into your home and then ignore him. If we had been there, would we have had the sense to sit at his feet, listen, and learn?

But this story isn't about two women in the year 30. It's about you and me right now. Here I sit, in a home with three Bibles, and how much time do I devote to listening to him through his word? I live in a town with perpetual adoration, and I don't know when I last went to sit in his presence.

Like Martha, I have God present in my home, in my community, and I ignore him. Like Martha, I am focused on tending to things that have little consequence and need to be reminded how and when I'm called to follow Christ, even in the midst of my daily tasks.

The Lord said to her in reply, "Martha, Martha, you are anxious and worried about many things. There is need of only one thing. Mary has chosen the better part and it will not be taken from her."
LUKE 10:41–42

When you lack courage to defend the Faith...

Saint Mary Zhu Wu

Mary Zhu Wu, a native of China, died a martyr's death in the Boxer Rebellion of 1900.

Recently, an acquaintance told a group of us a very disrespectful Catholic joke, to the apparent delight of all. I'd like to say that I spoke up with a voice of gentleness and wisdom. I'd even like to say that I spoke up with a voice of sharp rebuke. In truth, I did neither. I smiled and went on my way.

Many of us do the same on a daily basis. We have heard slander, derision, and ridiculous accusations about the Church. But rarely do we say anything at all. It's too awkward or difficult to stand up, to speak out.

Saint Mary Zhu Wu didn't find it awkward to stand up to protect what she knew to be sacred and true. During the Boxer Rebellion in China, the imperial army had joined forces with the Boxers to attack the Catholics of Mary's village. The soldiers stormed the church and found what they most wanted: two foreign-born priests. Immediately, Mary jumped up with arms outstretched to protect Father Leon Ignace Mangin. Both were killed instantly. Many more Catholics were slaughtered shortly thereafter.

Let us turn to Mary Zhu Wu and learn from her courageous example to leap to the defense of our faith and our God.

Be on your guard, stand firm in the faith, be courageous, be strong.
1 CORINTHIANS 16:13

When you feel like an outsider in the church...

Servant of God Dorothy Day

Dorothy Day (1897–1980) was the founder of the Catholic Worker movement. Her conversion after the birth of her daughter marked the beginning of a radically different life for Dorothy. She would devote herself entirely to caring for the poor, living with them in her Houses of Hospitality.

Have you ever felt that there are front-pew churchwomen, holy and devout, straight and narrow, and then there are the rest of us, more worldly, with shadier histories, shuffling into the back pew? If we view ourselves as the latter, then it's easy to feel that we don't have anything to contribute to our church. We think the "churchwomen" should tend to teaching, serving, organizing, and leading in our parish. We, on the other hand, aren't qualified. It's miracle enough that we duck in for Mass.

Servant of God Dorothy Day probably doesn't fit our picture of a churchwoman or an insider who was likely to set up and take on an important ministry. As a young woman in the 1920s, she led quite the scandalous life. She engaged in a series of love affairs, became pregnant, and had an abortion. She was briefly married to a man who had been married eight times. Later, she had a common-law marriage to an atheistic anarchist and became pregnant, this time deciding to have the baby.

It was during this pregnancy that Dorothy's powerful conversion began. Soon after her daughter's birth, both she and the baby were baptized.

And that was it. Dorothy was a new person. Her new life as a Christian became one entirely dedicated to serving the poor. She founded the newspaper *The Catholic Worker* and opened the first of many Houses of Hospitality, dedicated to sheltering the poor. Not only did Dorothy serve the poor, she lived with them in voluntary poverty.

Though she did not at all fit the "churchwoman" description, she lived as Christ, surrounding herself with those most in need, and dedicating herself to their service. Her example can help us imagine how the rest of us back-pew types may be called to serve God in the most surprising ways.

> So whoever is in Christ is a new creation: the old things
> have passed away; behold, new things have come.
> 2 CORINTHIANS 5:17

Dear Dorothy Day, please pray that I may follow your example and see myself as a new creation in Christ, a Christian who can and must contribute to her world.

When you struggle in prayer...

Saint Thérèse of Lisieux

Saint Thérèse of Lisieux is often affectionately called "the Little Flower." She only lived to the age of twenty-four and spent the last several years of her life as a cloistered Carmelite nun. However, her insights into prayer and her "little way" to holiness earned her the title Doctor of the Church. Saint Thérèse is the patron saint of missions. Her feast day is October 1.

As moms who are always on the go, we sometimes may find that our prayer lives have been reduced to cries of, "Help, Lord!" throughout the day. At some point, most of us feel as though our prayer life is stunted, empty, or imperfect in some way. Sometimes we may waste time wondering if we're praying in the "right" way. Or we may be so distracted during prayer that no words even come to mind. Or we may read beautiful prayers, but for all their eloquence, they don't express the desires or the anguish of our hearts.

When we begin to struggle in prayer, we could turn to Saint Thérèse of Lisieux. In her autobiography, Thérèse explained that she could not bring herself to "hunt through books for beautiful prayers." Instead, she said, "I behave like children who cannot read: I tell God very simply what I want and he always understands."

Approaching God in childlike simplicity may make all the difference in our prayers. Indeed, Jesus taught his disciples to begin their prayer with, "Our Father...." It is noteworthy that Jesus used the Aramaic term "Abba," which is not exactly the same as "Father." A better translation is "Papa" or "Daddy," terms that children use when calling on their fathers. So, if we begin our prayer with "Papa" and tell him all of our problems, and thank him for all of our blessings, let's do as Saint Thérèse and have faith that "he always understands."

"Let the children come to me; do not prevent them, for the kingdom of God belongs to such as these. Amen, I say to you, whoever does not accept the kingdom of God like a child will not enter it."
MARK 10:14–15

Saint Thérèse, please pray that I may approach our heavenly Father as simply and lovingly as a daughter approaches her daddy.

When you feel insecure about being Catholic...

Three Martyrs

All three of the following women were martyred simply for being Catholic. Each lived in a time of terrible persecution.

To say that Catholicism is unpopular in certain circles or areas may be an understatement. In some parts, any Christian religion is scorned. In other areas, the population may be largely Christian, but suspicious of Catholicism. In such circles, it may be easiest to keep a low profile, to not refer to our faith much, and to convince ourselves that it is a personal matter anyway.

When we are insecure about sharing our faith, we should consider the following martyrs, all of whom lived during times of outright persecution.

Blessed Tarsykia Olha Matskiv lived in the Ukraine from 1919–1944. Soviet forces were overrunning her country. One morning, Tarsykia was met at the convent gate by a Soviet soldier who shot and killed her. Why? He explained that it was simply because she was a nun.

Saint Lucy Pak Hui Sun of South Korea (1800–1839) was a lady-in-waiting to the queen at the royal court. She left her position in the court in order to learn more about Catholicism. She was soon baptized but soon was arrested for her beliefs. She was beaten severely in prison but refused to renounce her faith and was quickly decapitated.

Saint Magdalene of Nagasaki also lived in a time of persecution. She was raised by faithful Catholic parents who were martyred when Magdalene was twenty years old. When she was thirty-two, she lost, one-by-one, four spiritual directors to martyrdom. After the fourth one was killed, Magdalene decided to reveal her faith to government soldiers. She was hanged by her feet over a garbage pit until she died.

These women teach us that it is sometimes the simplest outward signs that witness to our faith, while at other times it is the courageous response under extreme pressure. In every situation, we are called to hold and share our faith without reservation.

I command you: be strong and steadfast! Do not fear nor be dismayed, for the LORD, your God, is with you wherever you go.
JOSHUA 1:9

Dear Saints Margaret and Lucy, and Blessed Tarsykia, each of you lived in a time of great persecution. Please pray that my fellow Catholics and I may appreciate the freedom we have to practice our faith and the courage to share it openly with others.

When suffering causes you to question your faith...

Saint Agnes

One of our earliest and youngest saints, Agnes lived in Rome from 292–305. She was martyred during Diocletian's reign. Her feast day is January 21, and she is the patron of engaged couples, virgins, rape victims, and chastity.

We're all familiar with the psalm about walking through the dark valley, or as some translations say, "the valley of the shadow of death." There are times when we know exactly what the psalmist meant, especially if we face any crisis involving our precious children. When we face our dark valley, we can begin to lose faith. When we do, we lose our strength and our peace, and the valley that was full of shadows becomes totally enveloped in darkness.

When we are going through our darkest hour and feel our faith slipping away, and our strength and peace quickly following, we can think of Saint Agnes. At the age of thirteen, she refused to worship Roman gods and was immediately sentenced to death. In the face of death, Agnes is recorded as being remarkably peaceful, showing no anxiety or fear right up to her execution. The source of this peace was her faith. She knew that heaven awaited, so there was nothing to fear.

Agnes' example of inner peace from steadfast faith should remind us that the same peace awaits us, even during our darkest hours.

> **The LORD is my shepherd; there is nothing I lack.…**
> **Even though I walk through the valley of the shadow of death,**
> **I will fear no evil, for you are with me.**
> PSALM 23:1 AND 4

Saint Agnes, your peaceful demeanor at the moment of your martyrdom was an outward sign of the intense faith you held. Please pray that my faith may fill me with courage and peace as I walk through the dark valleys in my own life.

When you feel enslaved by sin…

Saint Josephine Bakhita

Born in Sudan in 1869, Saint Josephine was kidnapped by slave traders at age seven. She was sold four times in the next ten years and suffered terrible abuse. Sold to an Italian family, she began her conversion experience while taking their daughter to catechism classes. After gaining her freedom, she became a nun and served as a homemaker in the convent until her death in 1947. Her feast day is February 8, and she is the patron of Sudan.

To what sin do you feel enslaved? Maybe it's an addiction or compulsive behavior you've wrestled with for years. Maybe it's a strong tendency toward unkindness to someone in your life. Whatever the case, know that through your baptism, you are no longer enslaved. In Romans 8:15, Saint Paul tells us, "For you did not receive a spirit of slavery to fall back into fear, but you received a spirit of adoption, through which we call 'Abba! Father!'"

Bakhita only knew slavery from a very young age. Eventually she ended up with an Italian family who treated her kindly and took her to Italy to look after their young daughter. After some time in Italy, the family planned to head back to Africa, but Bakhita refused to go. In an effort to force her to go, Bakhita's mistress took her to court. The plan backfired: the court ruled that since slavery was illegal in Italy, Bakhita had been free the whole time she had lived there. Free of the bonds of slavery, she embraced her freedom, which she knew she owed to God, and dedicated the rest of her life to his service.

When you begin to feel that snare that seeks to enslave you, call out, "Abba! Father!" to remind yourself that you are no longer a slave to sin, but a child of God.

We know that our old self was crucified with him, so that our sinful body might be done away with, that we might no longer be in slavery to sin.
ROMANS 6:6

Saint Josephine, you showed great strength and courage when you refused to be enslaved. Please pray for me that I may realize that I am a child of God, no longer a slave to sin.

When you feel hopeless...

Saint Rita of Cascia

A native of Italy, Saint Rita was born in 1381. Known as the patron of hopeless cases, Saint Rita met with many difficulties in life, but was faithful in prayer and charity. Her feast day is May 22.

We all feel hopeless about some area of our lives at some time or another. Maybe we've given up hope of ever redirecting our wayward child, improving our marriage, losing weight, or overcoming an addiction.

Saint Rita of Cascia is the patron saint of hopeless cases because she was quite familiar with seemingly hopeless situations in her own life. As a young girl, she desired to enter a convent, but her parents refused, insisting that she marry a wealthy man who would become an abusive husband. It was a hopeless state of affairs. After eighteen years of marriage, her husband was killed. Later, her two sons died in an epidemic, a hopelessly sad loss for any mother.

Rita then sought to enter the Augustinian Order, but was refused because she was a widow. Hopelessly rejected.

But then, a miracle: In a dream, John the Baptist, Saint Augustine and Saint Nicholas of Tolentine came to her and led her to the Augustinian convent. When Rita awoke, she was in the convent chapel. The prioress arrived, recognized the miracle and allowed Rita entrance to the order, where she remained faithful until her death.

Let us learn from Saint Rita, who clung to hope even when evidence mounted against it.

> **May the God of hope fill you with all joy and peace in believing, so that you may abound in hope by the power of the holy Spirit.**
> ROMANS 15:13

Dear Saint Rita, you faced disappointments, losses, and seemingly hopeless situations throughout your life. Please pray for me that I may remain faithful and hopeful as I face my own difficulties and setbacks in this life.

When you are consumed with vanity...

Saint Rose of Lima

A native of Peru, Saint Rose lived from 1586–1617. She was prohibited by her parents from entering the convent, so she lived at home as a member of the Third Order of Saint Dominic. Her life was one of penance, solitude and service. Saint Rose of Lima is the patron saint of the Philippines, Peru, Latin America, South America, and florists.

Eyebrow lifts, facials, hair coloring, manicures, pedicures, designer clothes, and handbags. We need it all!

Every day it seems we're bombarded with ads telling us that there is something else we need to do to make ourselves more attractive. While it's great to want to look our best, primping, perfecting, and purchasing new products can become an obsession. We waste our time, money, and energy pursuing an unrealistic notion of what we should be. Worse yet, we can begin to judge our worth and gain our identity by how good we look, and then judge others in the same way.

Before we get too carried away, we might think about a saint who went to the other extreme.

An attractive girl, Saint Rose of Lima is known for rubbing pepper on her lovely face in order to mar her beauty. Today no one would recommend that we purposely destroy the natural beauty that God has given us. However, maybe just remembering Rose's practice can help us recall that our identity is not tied up in our appearance. Saint Paul tells us our true identity: "In Christ Jesus you are all children of God through faith...." And that's beautiful.

**Charm is deceptive, and beauty fleeting;
the woman who fears the Lord is to be praised.**
PROVERBS 31:30

When you are afraid to answer God's call...

Blessed Mother—the Annunciation

"'Hail, favored one! The Lord is with you!' But she was greatly troubled at what was said and pondered what sort of greeting this might be. Then the angel said to her, 'Do not be afraid, Mary, for you have found favor with God'" (Luke 1:28–30).

Troubled and afraid. Such was Mary's response to Archangel Gabriel's arrival.

Upon first encountering the great plan God has for us, we may feel the same way. Troubled, we may first wonder, "Uh-oh. What is this about?" Whatever we are being called to can cause an upheaval, a change, a challenge. And then we begin to feel afraid, thinking of all that can go wrong, all the reasons we may fail.

What to do then? Read further to Luke 1:38. Once Mary understood her role in God's plan, she responded, "Behold, I am the handmaid of the Lord. May it be done to me according to your word."

There is our ultimate model for following God's will. We can be troubled or frightened for a moment, but only for a moment. Once our mission is clear to us, we can follow Mary's example, for we too, are handmaids of the Lord.

Trust in the LORD with all your heart, on your own intelligence do not rely; In all your ways be mindful of him.
PROVERBS 3:5–6

Mary, Mother of God, you gave us a beautiful model of how to respond in faith to the Lord's call. Please pray for me that I may never remain too troubled or afraid to respond in faith and confidence.